MARRIAGE FOR THE BETTER

A Biblical Guide to a God-designed Marriage

MARCIA J. ESTRADA

Unless otherwise indicated, all Scripture quotations are taken from the *King James Version* of the Bible.

Scriptures marked NKJV are taken from the NEW KING JAMES VERSION (NKJV): Scripture taken from the NEW KING JAMES VERSION®. Copyright© 1982 by Thomas Nelson, Inc. Used by permission. All rights reserved.

Scripture quotations marked NIV are taken from the HOLY BIBLE, NEW INTERNATIONAL VERSION®. NIV®. Copyright © 1973, 1978, 1984 by International Bible Society. Used by permission of Zondervan. All rights reserved worldwide.

Scripture quotations marked AMP taken from the Amplified® Bible, Copyright © 1954, 1958, 1962, 1964, 1965, 1987 by The Lockman Foundation Used by permission.

Scriptures marked TLB are taken from the THE LIVING BIBLE (TLB): Scripture taken from THE LIVING BIBLE copyright© 1971. Used by permission of Tyndale House Publishers, Inc., Carol Stream, Illinois 60188. All rights reserved.

Scriptures marked RSV are taken from the REVISED STANDARD VERSION (RSV): Scripture taken from the REVISED STANDARD VERSION, Grand Rapids: Zondervan, 1971.

Marriage for the Better
A Biblical Guide to a God-designed Marriage
ISBN-13:
978-1976578250
ISBN-10:
1976578256

Copyright © 2017 by Marcia Estrada

Published by
Ashley Estrada Ministries
Kissimmee, FL
www.ashleyestradaministries.com

All rights reserved. No part of this book may be reproduced or transmitted in any form or by any means without written permission of the author
All rights reserved.

This book is dedicated to

My husband, Apostle Ashley C Estrada

With him, I have truly experienced being married, for the better.

He is my best friend and my encourager, who for over 38 years, has never failed to make me know that I

am completely loved.

If I had it to do all over again, there is no one I would want to call my husband, other than him.

CONTENTS

    Acknowledgments   i

1. Why Marry?   3
   "When you realize you want to spend the rest of your life with somebody, you want the rest of your life to start as soon as possible."
   — When Harry Met Sally

2. It's Not About You   15
   "Love is that condition in which the happiness of another person is essential to your own."
   — Robert Heinlein

3. Contract or Covenant   23
   "Lots of people want to ride with you in the limo, but what you want is someone who will take the bus with you when the limo breaks down."
   — Oprah Winfrey

4. Love in any Language   35
   They do not love that do not show their love.
   — William Shakespeare

5. The Head, The Tail, and the Edge   45
   "You don't love someone because they're perfect; you love them in spite of the fact that they're not."
   — Jodi Picoult

6. Family Matters   57
   You don't choose your family. They are God's gift to you, as you are to them.
   — Desmond Tutu

7. Money Matters Too   67
   "You don't love someone for their looks, or their clothes or for their fancy car, but because they sing a song only you can hear."
   — Oscar Wilde

8. Who's the Boss?   79
   Marriage, in its truest sense, is a partnership of equals, with neither exercising dominion over the other, but, rather, with each encouraging and assisting the other in whatever responsibilities and aspirations he or she might have.
   — Gordon B. Hinckley

9	**Who's First?**	93
	"When we put God first, all other things fall into their proper place or drop out of our lives. Our love of the Lord will govern the claims for our affection, the demands on our time, the interests we pursue, and the order of our priorities." — Ezra Taft Benson	
10	**Don't Make Out, Make Love**	105
	It is not a lack of love, but a lack of friendship that makes unhappy marriages. — Friedrich Nietzsche	
11	**Love is a Verb**	115
	"Think not because you are now wed, that all your courtship's at an end." — Antonio Hurtado de Mendoza	
12	**For the Better**	123
	"When marrying, ask yourself this question: Do you believe that you will be able to converse well with this person into your old age? Everything else in marriage is transitory." — Friedrich Nietzsche	

ACKNOWLEDGEMENTS

This book is a testimony of the devotion to excellence of my son, Pastor Kenneth Estrada, who labored countless hours over every page to ensure that it was formatted in a pleasant and appealing way and who also designed the cover. I am also thankful to my sister, Yvonne Duncan who did the first proofreading.

I am grateful to the many couples who have trusted me to counsel with them before marriage and to those who came to me when their marriages were in danger.

Most of all, I thank the Lord Jesus Christ who has counted me faithful in putting me into the ministry, and entrusting me with a ministry of reconciliation.

"God has given us the exciting privilege of working together with Him to raise generations..."

chapter 01

WHY MARRY?

By all means marry. If you get a good wife, you'll be happy. If you get a bad one, you'll become a philosopher...and that is a good thing for any man. – Socrates

My husband and I got married when we were twenty-four years old and began to lead a small congregation, in a small village, on a small island. I remember that our new neighbor asked us why we married at such a young age. That question surprised me, because in my mind, twenty-four was not young.

I remember as a young person growing up fantasizing

about the man I would marry and what my wedding ceremony would be like. Today even though weddings continue, many young people are fearful of marriage.

My daughter and I got into a very intense argument one day. "But what's wrong with living together with someone before you marry them? Isn't it better to find out before you get married whether you really want to be with this person for the rest of your life?" she asked.

Her argument sounded so reasonable. I was frustrated because I felt she should know better. After all, she had been raised as a "pastor's kid". Her father and I had been happily married all those years. Why should I have to explain something so fundamental to her?

But my daughter's dilemma was not unique. I have discovered that many young people raised in Christian homes are deviating from what they learned in church and argue that it makes sense to live together with someone before you marry that person. They have seen so many failed marriages of parents, church members, pastors, movie stars, well-known television personalities, and political leaders, that they are afraid to marry lest they become a statistic along the way. So, they relegate marriage to the same category as a new automobile purchase and want to go on a "practice drive" before they commit to the purchase.

Yet the Word of God clearly states ***"Marriage is honorable among all, and the bed undefiled; but fornicators and adulterers God will judge." Hebrews 13:4***

It appears that God has a divine interest in marriage. In the beginning, God institutionalized marriage between one man and one woman. This was His blueprint, His original plan that He expected would be copied by the rest of His children.

As a biblical counselor, my favorite activity is pre-marital counseling. I like to get into the ring with them before they mess up, rather than with the married couple who left wounds to fester until an amputation seems to be the only way out.

I usually tell couples. "Do not set a date until we have completed the counseling sessions". I don't recommend and don't like to be pressured into counseling a couple a few weeks before their wedding. I reason that if during the counseling, they discover that to go through with the marriage would be a disaster waiting to happen, they may be unwilling to postpone or to cancel the wedding because of the financial and emotional investments that have already been made and the embarrassment that they will face.

But let's go back to the very beginning, the genesis of the

marriage relationship. God made a man, gave him a job (to be the keeper of a garden) and made him sovereign over all God's other creatures. In fact, God brought every animal to the man to see what the man would call it and whatever the man called it, became its name. But, the book of Genesis says: **"The man gave names to all livestock and to the birds of the heavens and to every beast of the field. But for Adam there was not found a helper fit for him." Genesis 2:20 ESV**

This parade of the animals had been prompted by God's observation that it was not good that the man should be alone and that He, God, would make a helper for the man. Here is the rationale for marriage. We should marry because **IT IS NOT GOOD TO BE ALONE.**

God's first purpose for instituting marriage is to deal with the problem of aloneness. *The American Heritage Dictionary of the English Language* defines alone as "Being apart from others; solitary; being without anyone or anything else; only, considered separately from all others of the same class. Being without equal; unique". *The New Thesaurus Roget's 11,* adds synonyms such as "unique, only, single, lone, solitary, one and only", and "by yourself, independently, unaided, unaccompanied, without help, on your own, unassisted, without assistance, under your own steam".

IT'S NOT GOOD TO BE ALONE

I want to zone in on two of these definitions "being without equal, unique as well as "unaided, without help, on your own." I believe this is exactly what prompted God to provide a wife for Adam and He proved this by parading all the animals in front of Adam. But Adam was one of a kind, he was unique. God had given him a job but there was no one to help him. He was on his own. That's why God designed marriage. He did not want the male man to be the only one of his kind or species (one made in the image and likeness of God Himself) but He wanted him to find companionship with the female "man" that had been taken out of him. Primarily, God designed marriage so that mankind would have companionship with another being like himself or herself, one equal to himself or herself, *of the same class or species as himself or herself but different to him or her, sexually, so that the species would continue.*

THE GUY NEEDS HELP!!!

Secondarily, God designed marriage so that the man He created would have help. Now some may argue that marriage is not necessary for those two requisites to be satisfied. Many who live together without being married find companionship with one another. Many also find the help that they want in the person with whom they are co-habiting.

Therefore, why should we even bother to marry?

Well, Adam himself answered the question. When God performed the first surgery upon man, gave him an anesthesia (caused a deep sleep to fall upon the man) (Genesis 2:21), removed one of his ribs, closed its place with flesh, made a woman and brought her to the man, Adam's response was, **"This at last is bone of my bones and flesh of my flesh; she shall be called Woman because she was taken out of Man". Genesis 2:23 (ESV).**

The writer of Genesis then states **"THEREFORE, or, for this reason, a man shall leave his father and his mother and hold fast (cleave) to his wife, and they shall become one flesh". Genesis 2:24 (ESV)**

This is the essence of marriage. This is selection. This is an act of will, a demonstration of one of the attributes of man, that a man can select one woman, out of many, to become one flesh with him, to complete him, and to have her share with him, the rib that was taken from him.

This is a formal, official act found in many cultures, where a man LEAVES the closest relationship he has had before this time, that of his father and particularly his mother (out of whose body he has come), to join himself to someone who was a stranger to him, unknown, from another family, and possibly from a different culture.

Through the act of marriage, he comes into union and oneness with that person and must hold fast, or stick to or cleave to or remain with her for the rest of their earthly lives. That, my friends, is marriage. That is what is meant by the word marry. That is the promise that is evoked when a man promises to "forsake all others, and cleave only to her as long as we both shall live." This is so powerful. There is so much spiritual significance in this, that it is no wonder that this institution, established by God, has come under such violent attacks.

MAKE MORE OF YOU

Thirdly, God gave the man and woman a mandate to reproduce. If we go back to Genesis 1:27 & 28, we read the headlines of the story that later followed. We see that **"God created man in his own image, in the image of God he created him; male and female he created them." (ESV)**

"And God blessed them and God said to them, 'Be fruitful and multiply and fill the earth and subdue it and have dominion over the fish of the sea and over the birds of the heavens and over every living thing that moves on the earth.'

The species man, is male and female, created in God's image. God's mandate to them was to reproduce after their kind_ to make more men and women in the image and likeness of God, to behave like God, by ruling and dominating every other living thing upon the earth and even the earth itself.

God's intention was to produce a godly seed. This is something that God wanted from the beginning. So when the first Adam messed up, God sent the last Adam (Jesus, the Christ) to fulfill what Adam had failed to do.

Hebrews 2:13 quotes Jesus saying **"Here am I and the children God has given me"**.

Malachi 2:15 reiterates this desire of God for more children.

Didn't the LORD make you one with your wife? In body and spirit, you are his. And what does he want? Godly children from your union. So, guard your heart; remain loyal to the wife of your youth. NLT

In Genesis 18:17 – 19, when God was about to bring judgment upon Sodom and Gomorrah because of the wickedness of the people, He decided to let Abraham in on His intentions because of one factor, He knew that Abraham would raise His offspring in the ways of the Lord.

> *"Then the Lord said, Shall I hide from Abraham what I am about to do? Abraham will surely become a great and powerful nation, and all nations on earth will be blessed through him. For I have chosen him, so that he will direct his children and his household after him to keep the way of the Lord by doing what*

is right and just, so that the Lord will bring about for Abraham what he has promised him."
-Genesis 18:17-19 (NIV)

The New Testament echoes this theme in 1 Corinthians 7:14 *"For the unbelieving husband has been sanctified through his wife, and the unbelieving wife has been sanctified through her believing husband. Otherwise your children would be unclean, but as it is, they are holy." (NIV)*

In His infinite wisdom, God knew that the most efficient and effective way of multiplying His Seed, godly Seed, was to utilize the family unit. He decided to partner with married couples to have them raise up children and teach them the ways of the Lord so thoroughly, that generations would be affected for good.

Therefore, we SHOULD marry. God has given us the exciting privilege of working together with Him to raise generations, a godly lineage stretching from the beginning of the earth into eternity of those He can call His children, who love Him and call Him, Daddy.

REVIEW:

1) List 3 reasons why we should marry.

   _____

   _____

   _____

2) Why is God depending upon Christian parents to raise godly seed, what does He ultimately want?

   _____

3) Why do you want to get married? Or why did you marry?

   _____

   _____

4) List 3 Qualities you have seen in your fiancé or spouse that contributed to you wanting to marry him or her.

   _____

   _____

   _____

5) List 3 Things about yourself that you feel has contributed to your fiancé or spouse wanting to marry you.

   _____

   _____

   _____

"Because of your demonstration of Christ and the Church in your marriage, you can raise up a generation of God lovers instead of God haters..."

IT'S NOT ABOUT YOU

"In every marriage, more than a week old, there are grounds for divorce. The trick is to find, and continue to find, grounds for marriage." ~ Robert Anderson, Solitaire & Double Solitaire

Engaged couples are usually startled when I tell them "This marriage is not about you".

"How can you say that?" they ask. "We are the ones who fell in love with each other and who are financing our wedding. How can you say it's not about us?"

Let me shock you even further. I tell married couples on

the brink of divorce who come to me for counsel, that it's not about them. "How can you say that?" they ask. "I'm the one that's hurting". "My wife does not respect me". "My husband shows no affection to me. How can you say it's not about me?"

Please hear me out. I'm in no way trying to minimize the trauma that some people are experiencing in their marriage and despite what I am about to say, I am not advocating that a man and woman should remain together at any cost. However, I'm about to share with you something that I believe God shared with me as I spoke with couples over the years.

In the Book of Ephesians, chapter 5, the apostle Paul writes:

> *Husbands, love your wives, just as Christ loved the church and gave himself up for her to make her holy, cleansing her by the washing with water through the word, and to present her to himself as a radiant church, without stain or wrinkle or any other blemish, but holy and blameless. In this same way, husbands ought to love their wives as their own bodies. He who loves his wife loves himself. After all, no one ever hated their own body, but they feed and care for their body, just as Christ does the church— for we are members of his body. "For this reason a man will leave his father and mother and be united to his wife, and the two will become one flesh." This is a profound mystery—but I am talking about Christ and the church. However, each one of you also must love his wife as he loves himself, and the wife must respect her husband.*
> *- Ephesians 5:25-33 NIV*

The apostle talks about a mystery. In fact, he calls it "a profound" or a great, or a deep, hidden mystery. This mystery is the fact that a man will leave his parents, cleave to his wife and two shall become one. But then in the same breath Paul says "but I'm talking about Christ and the church". From verse 25 to verse 32, Paul vacillates between talking about the husband and wife relationship and the relationship between Christ and the church.

I always get excited when I talk about this! Here it is that when God wanted to describe the relationship, the sacrificial love, the voluntary submission, the oneness that exists between His Son, Jesus Christ and His Son's bride, the body of born-again believers, God could find no other illustration to describe that relationship but the one that should exist between a man and his wife!

It's not just about you! God designed marriage. His blueprint of it was intended to be a replica of the relationship between His Son, whom He loves, and the Church, whom He equally loves.

Every time someone sees a man and his wife interacting with each other, if they have never heard about Jesus and His love for the church, they should be seeing a "reality show" exemplifying that. That's why the apostle Paul describes the sacrificial love of Jesus in giving His life for the church in the same breath as the sacrificial love that the husband should have for his wife.

SHE BLOOMS IN YOUR GARDEN

A man's relationship with his wife should result in her growth as a person (holy, blameless, without stain or wrinkle, radiant). She blooms in his garden. A man should nourish, cherish, and treat his wife with tenderness to the extent that he also takes care of his own body. When a man does this, the wife should most naturally respect her husband. This is what Christ did and does for the church and this is the way the church is expected to respond to Christ.

Your marriage then is not just about you. When you choose to take offense and to belittle and abuse and disrespect each other, you are a distorted picture of Christ and His Church. My mother used to say to my children, "Remember you may be the only Bible that someone may read". When your son and your daughter "read" your marriage, what is it telling them?

The challenge is this. Our flesh craves justification. We have an inordinate need to be right. We are quick to take offense. Our focus is on what my husband or my wife should be doing for me instead of what can I do for him or her? We harbor unforgiveness and go to bed angry at each other contrary to the scripture that says it's okay to be angry but we should not go to bed angry with each other because anger, when it is prolonged, becomes sinful.

Be angry and do not sin; on your bed, reflect in your heart and be still.
- Ephesians 4:24 HSCB

IT'S GENERATIONAL

It's not about you. It's about the generations that are in you, the children who are yet to be born from your children, grand-children, great-grand-children and the rest of your lineage. Do you realize that their lives may be negatively affected because of the decision you are making to leave rather that cleave, to hurt rather than heal, to seek revenge instead of reconciliation, to betray rather than to be faithful? What difference might it make, if because of your demonstration of Christ and the Church in your marriage, you can raise up a generation of God lovers instead of God haters?

One of the things we need to understand is this. Whatever our children see modeled is going to have a tremendous impact upon them one way or the other. Separation and divorce of parents affect children to the extent that some of them become fearful and distrustful of entering marriage. Some of them marry but then they act out the very behaviors that led to the divorce of their parents. Psychological factors come into play and result in some children gravitating to men or women who display the same negative behaviors that their parents displayed. Consequently, the spirit of divorce passes on to another generation.

What difference might it make if God could say of you as He said of Abraham **"For I have chosen him, so that he will direct his children and his household after him to keep the way of the LORD by doing what is right and just"**? *(Genesis 18:19 NIV)*

Did you believe that marriage is a costume party for you to dress up as Cinderella and Prince Charming and live happily ever after? I'm sorry to be the one to disillusion you, but it's not about you after all. God had a whole lot more in mind when He decided to allow you and me to collaborate with Him in this institutionalized relationship that we call marriage.

REVIEW

Read Ephesians 5: 22-36

1. *List all the action words that describe how a husband should relate to his wife.*

   _____

   _____

   _____

2. *List all the action words that describe how a wife should respond to her husband.*

   _____

   _____

   _____

3. *What is the mystery that the Apostle Paul revealed?*

   _____

   _____

   _____

4. *On a scale of 1 – 10, 1 being the least and 10 being the most, what grade will you give your relationship if we were to use it as an example of the relationship of Christ and the church?* _____

"Covenant supersedes contract because covenant is how God deals with us."

chapter 03

CONTRACT OR COVENANT

Wife: "What are you doing?" Husband: Nothing. Wife: "Nothing...? You've been reading our marriage certificate for an hour." Husband: "I was looking for the expiration date."

We live in such a litigious society that wise people have learned the value of making contracts when entering business deals with other individuals. It is very sad that no longer is a person's word a guarantee. We have become accustomed to signing contracts as a way of life.

I'm not good at telling jokes but I thought I just had to

share this one, which I recently saw online, with you:

> One day in Contract Law class, the professor asked one of his better students, "Now if you were to give someone an orange, how would you go about it?"
> The student replied, "Here's an orange."
> The professor was livid. "No! No! Think like a lawyer!"
> The student then recited, "Okay, I'd tell him, 'I hereby give and convey to you all and singular, my estate and interests, rights, claim, title, claim and advantages of and in, said orange, together with all its rind, juice, pulp, and seeds, and all rights and advantages with full power to bite, cut, freeze and otherwise eat, the same, or give the same away with and without the pulp, juice, rind and seeds, anything herein before or hereinafter or in any deed, or deeds, instruments of whatever nature or kind whatsoever to the contrary in anywise notwithstanding..."

We sign a contract for our cell phone plans. We sign a contract when we rent or lease an apartment or house. We sign a contract when we purchase a vehicle. We sign a contract when we lend or borrow money. We sign a contract when we employ someone or are employed by someone. These are just a few everyday events when we enter legal and binding contracts with other individuals.

All of us have probably heard the term "breach of

contract" which is the term used when one party or the other reneges on the terms and conditions of the contract that they entered into with one another. Some of you might even have experienced the trauma of having lost money or your good name because you signed a contract without fully understanding the terms of the contract or because you didn't seek legal advice before you signed your name.

I say all of this to point out the fact that we are "contract-minded" and that because we are "contract-minded", we tend to enter marriage with the idea that because we have signed a legal document, we have a contract with our spouse. Consequently, many marriages operate at contract level, if not in all areas, at least in one.

I have had couples come before me whose marriages are failing because the other party has reneged on the unwritten financial contract.

"I pay all the utility bills and the grocery bill, why is it so hard for him to pay the rent on time?" Or, "My wife always has money for another pair of shoes but she never has money to help with any of the bills!"

For some couples, the battle is over the division of labor. One or the other, or both, feel as though the other person is not keeping the unwritten contract concerning who does what.

Because my love language (see more on this in the next chapter) is acts of service, I used to feel unloved if I was left to do most of the household chores. We hear so many complaints from wives who argue that since they are out working during the same hours that their husbands are, it is unfair for husbands to come home and expect to sit in front of the television while their wives cook dinner.

Even when the wife is a stay-at-home mom, she feels that at the end of the day, she should be able to get help from her husband who has had the benefit of being out of the house all day. She argues that she is exhausted from having had to care for children and do household chores all day.

The story is told of a husband who came home one evening and found the house in total disarray, laundry not done, dishes unwashed, no dinner, house in an uproar, so he hurried to his wife to ask her what happened. Nonchalantly, she responded, "Nothing", she said, "But you usually ask me when you get home what I did all day, so today I just decided not to do any of those things that I do all day".

Husbands on the other hand, who have very physical jobs or who come from backgrounds where the men in the family were not expected to do household chores, feel very offended when their wives fuss about the fact that they are not helping. "A man's home is his castle" he says, "when I get home I just want to put my feet up and relax".

So, the expectation is there. We have a contract. If I pay the utilities, you should pay the groceries. If I wash the laundry, you should at least fold them and put them away.

BUT IT'S NOT A CONTRACT

I feel what you feel. I can empathize with what so many of you are going through right now. I believe that we should play fair. But I must let you know that marriage is not a contract. Marriage is a covenant. But isn't that the same thing? No. NO. God never uses the expression contract in the context of marriage. He uses the word covenant both to the man and the woman.

> **Wisdom will save you from the immoral woman, from the seductive words of the promiscuous woman. She has abandoned her husband and ignores the covenant she made before God.**
> **- Proverbs 2:16 – 17 (NLT)**

> **Another thing you do: You flood the Lord's altar with tears. You weep and wail because he no longer looks with favor on your offerings or accepts them with pleasure from your hands. You ask, "Why?" It is because the Lord is the witness between you**

and the wife of your youth. You have been unfaithful to her, though she is your partner, the wife of your marriage covenant.
- *Malachi 2:13 – 14 (NIV)*

Both references illustrate that as far as the One who instituted marriage is concerned, marriage is no contract, it is a covenant. Moreover, He takes covenant seriously. I mean He is so serious about it that He says even if you cry, I don't want anything from you because you have broken covenant with the wife of your youth.

This is heavy stuff. But just in case you are saying this is all Old Testament or Old Covenant, let's look at what is said under the New Covenant.

Married men, in the same way, live with your wives with a clear recognition of the fact that they are weaker than you. Yet, since you are heirs with them of God's free gift of Life, treat them with honor; so that your prayers may not be hindered. 1 Peter 3:7 (Weymouth Translation)

Men, doesn't this sound just like what we read in Malachi, that God is not listening to you and will not answer your prayers if you are not honoring the covenant relationship between you and your wife?

COVENANT IS SERIOUS

You see covenant is serious. Covenant supersedes contract because covenant is how God deals with us. God was so serious about covenant that He didn't even spare His Son, but delivered Him up freely for all of us. (Romans 8:32). Every time we open the New Testament, we are reading the New Covenant.

Covenant is not a fifty-fifty affair. It is each party giving one hundred percent. It involves one or the other continuing to give one hundred percent even when the other party might have stopped giving one hundred percent.

Covenant is not a light thing. It usually involves the shedding of blood. Some of us may have watched movies in which we saw people from different tribes cutting themselves and allowing their blood to flow together so that they could become "blood brothers". Once this act had taken place, they were obligated to come to the help and defense of each other whenever the need arose.

The act of intercourse initiated a blood covenant between a husband and wife. In the couple's first sexual experience, the virgin husband would enter his virgin wife and as this took place, her hymen would be broken and blood would flow. They then became "one flesh", joined in covenant together by God Himself and not to be separated by man.

We have messed up. We have taken this holy act outside of the parameters that God established through premarital sex, extramarital sex, and perverted sexual behavior. We have legislated behaviors that God has not and will not sanction. The apostle Paul describes the condition of mankind given up and given over by their Creator. His description is as relevant to our 21st century as much as it was relevant in A.D. 56 – 57 when it was written.

> *Therefore God gave them over in the sinful desires of their hearts to sexual impurity for the degrading of their bodies with one another. They exchanged the truth about God for a lie, and worshiped and served created things rather than the Creator— who is forever praised. Amen. Because of this, God gave them over to shameful lusts. Even their women exchanged natural sexual relations for unnatural ones. In the same way the men also abandoned natural relations with women and were inflamed with lust for one another. Men committed shameful acts with other men, and received in themselves the due penalty for their error. Furthermore, just as they did not think it worthwhile to retain the knowledge of God, so God gave them over to a depraved mind, so that they do what ought not to be done. They have become filled with every kind of wickedness, evil, greed and depravity. They are full of envy, murder, strife, deceit and malice. They are gossips, slanderers, God-haters, insolent, arrogant and boastful; they invent ways of doing evil;*

they disobey their parents; they have no understanding, no fidelity, no love, no mercy. Although they know God's righteous decree that those who do such things deserve death, they not only continue to do these very things but also approve of those who practice them.
- Romans 1:24 – 32 (NIV)

When we examine these verses of the Bible in the light of covenant, understanding the value that God places on covenant, we can understand God's vexation with mankind. At the same time, we are overwhelmed by His love that would allow Him to send His Son to bear the punishment for our wrong-doings.

In Romans 5:7 and 8, Paul says that someone would hardly die for a righteous man, but sometimes some people will dare to die for a good man, but God proved His love toward us, in that "while we were yet sinners, Christ died for us" and ushered in the New Covenant between God and man.

When we understand the seriousness of covenant, we will not set aside our spouses easily. We will fight to preserve our marriages and the future of our children. We will fight to preserve marriage as God defined it because it helps to hold together the very fabric of society.

REVIEW

1. *Give an example of a couple who you think are in a covenant relationship with each other. What characteristics do you see in them that makes you feel so?*

   _____

   _____

   _____

2. *Examine your relationship with your fiancé or spouse. In what ways, have you been operating under contract principles? What would you change to bring your relationship in line with covenant principles?*

   _____

   _____

   _____

3. *What is your opinion about pre-nuptial agreements? Do you believe they are harmful or helpful to marriages?*

   _____

   _____

   _____

"...if we want to save our marriages, we must save not just money in the bank but we must save those behaviors that matter to our spouses."

LOVE IN ANY LANGUAGE

A wife was looking at herself in the mirror and said "I feel fat, old and ugly. I really need a compliment from you right now". Her husband responded, "you have perfect eyesight".

I remember the first time I read the book, *The Five Love Languages* by Gary Chapman. It was as though he had opened a door of revelation and allowed me to walk in. This book is a "must read" for anyone who is serious about relationships.

In his book, Gary Chapman describes the way people show love and receive love. He talks about five love languages:

Words of affirmation

Physical touch

Quality time and conversation

Gifts

Acts of service

Even though Mr. Chapman's book has become a best seller and he has since written many others, there are still many people who are unfamiliar with his teaching.

Basically, he proposes that different people have different ways of expressing love and that if love is not shown to them in the same way, they can go through life feeling that they are not loved. In fact those closest to them were showing them love all the time but in a way that they did not know to interpret as love.

My husband and I were born in two different nations. His primary language is English, but he also spoke "patois" which has many elements of the French language while not being truly French. He could say "I love you" to me in patois but I did not know what he was saying. Until I learned the phrase myself, and knew what it meant, it meant nothing to me. We were in Bible School together and he would deliberately say things to me or about me in his other language.

His friends would laugh but I did not know what he said until one of them would interpret. This made our courtship very interesting and romantic to me but if he had only expressed his love in a language I did not understand, it would be of no benefit or comfort to me.

Similarly, people have different love languages. They express love and receive love in their love language. My love language is acts of service. When people voluntarily help me, thus conserving my time and energy, I am naturally drawn to them. Before my husband understood this about me, he did not know why I would be upset when he turned over some task that I had asked him to do to someone else. I would say to him, "When I ask you to do something for me, even if it's something as simple as making me a cup of tea, please don't call one of the children to do it for me".

When he delegated the task to someone else, I felt as though he was saying that it was an inconvenience to him. My female mind translated this to mean he did not love me.

One of the main ways I express my love to him and to my children up to this day, is by acts of service. I do not love cooking but I love cooking for them.

When any member of my family returns from a trip, I spare no effort in making the house and their rooms inviting for their return. Now this may not matter to them. But it means a lot to me. It means I am happy that you are coming home and so I prepared for you.

I don't usually travel without my husband. But I remember traveling to another state many years ago, and coming back home to meet the house in disarray. To this day, I cannot verbalize or explain how I felt. That experience was so significant that I remember the exact spot in the house where I stood and how I felt at the time. Praise God we all continue to grow and my husband has never allowed me to experience something like that again.

He, on the other hand, expresses love by words of affirmation and physical touch. I have never lacked for compliments and verbal validation by my husband. I have never lacked for hugs and other demonstrations of affection from him. Yet this area has been my area for growth. As a child, I was always fearful of expressing love verbally and I was also reluctant to touch or be touched. It is a testimony to God's grace and my husband's love and godly example, that I have grown in that area. And it is also a testimony that while we may speak different languages of love, if we are willing to focus on our spouse's needs, we will have a long and happy married life.

I remember one young lady who came to me very hurt and even angry because her husband did not make any effort to buy her gifts on special occasions. Her love language was gifts. She expressed her love by giving to others. She exerted herself to make sure that he was taken care of on birthdays, Fathers' Day, and Christmas. She felt that at the very least, he should reciprocate. She wanted him to make the effort to purchase a gift that would wow her on their wedding anniversary and on her birthday. Giving her money at the end of the day was an afterthought. She wanted to know that he remembered and that the day mattered to him as much as it mattered to her.

He, on the other hand, while he did not return the gifts she gave him, was very nonchalant about it all and did not consider it much of "a big deal". His mistake was that he did not understand that it was "a big deal" to his wife and that in not reciprocating, he could have done permanent damage to his relationship. Thankfully, they are still happily married today because one or both made some adjustments.

IS THERE ANY LOVE LEFT IN THE BANK?

As a biblical counselor, I have had many opportunities to counsel with couples struggling with feeling unappreciated or unloved. Many times, their feelings are deceiving them. The problem is that the other party is failing to express love in a way that can be interpreted as love. For example, let's say that one spouse's love language is quality time and quality conversation. This is how the session may go when the wife is the one who needs quality conversation, "He comes home and just sits in front of the television. He does not talk about what his day was like or ask me about my day."

"We don't go anywhere together Pastor Marcia, but when we were courting he was not like that, we would talk for hours and we were always going somewhere or doing something together".

What happened? Well, her love bank was being filled up by quality time and talk during courtship but now her husband has not been making frequent deposits and she is beginning to experience love bankruptcy.

Sometimes it is the husband who feels cheated. "She used to love to watch football with me, she even went to the games with me, now all she wants to do is to go shopping. I hate malls!" What happened? She showed love to him during courtship by doing the things with him that he loved, but no one told her that to keep him feeling loved, she needs to keep on doing those things. Now he wonders what happened to the woman he married.

I know part of the problem is that life gets in the way. New responsibilities involving children and work can seriously affect those whose love language involves taking and making time to talk and to do things together recreationally. But if we want to save our marriages, we must save not just money in the bank but we must save those behaviors that matter to our spouses.

Those things that matter to our spouses are keys to building strong relationships that weather the storms of life and stand the test of time.

Gary Chapman posits the view that love has several languages. The problem is that we don't all speak the same "lovingalese" (my word for love language). However, if we are to be successful in our marriage or in any relationship, we must discern the other person's way of expressing and receiving love and make every effort to see to it that he or she is not running on empty. We must stop being selfish and practice valuing our spouses.

> ***Philippians 2: 2 – 5 make my joy complete by being like-minded, having the same love, being one in spirit and of one mind. 3 Do nothing out of selfish ambition or vain conceit. Rather, in humility value others above yourselves, 4 not looking to your own interests but each of you to the interests of the others.5 In your relationships with one another, have the same mindset as Christ Jesus:***

REVIEW

1. *What is your primary and secondary love language?*
   _____

2. *Which of those listed, makes you angry or hurt when it is withheld from you?*
   _____

3. *What is your fiancé's or spouse's primary love language?*
   _____

4. *In the last week, how have you attempted to let your fiancé or spouse know that you love him/her?*
   _____
   _____
   _____
   _____

5. *If you have not done so yet, Read Gary Chapman's <u>Five Love Languages</u> and be certain to identify the love languages of those around you.*

"Characteristics that you see in a person before you marry, qualities that you do not like, will be magnified under the microscope of marriage."

chapter 05

THE HEAD, THE TAIL, AND THE EDGE

After a lengthy quarrel, Mandy said to her husband, Dave, 'You know, I was a fool when I married you.' Dave replied quickly, 'Yes, Mandy, but I was in love and didn't notice it.'

Has someone ever attempted to trick you by tossing a coin and saying "If it's the head I win, if it's the tail you lose"? It took me a while as a child to figure out that in a scenario like that, the person at the other end, namely me, was always the loser and the person throwing out the challenge was always the winner.

It took me a while also to realize that when we talk about a person's strengths and weaknesses, it is a paradox. Usually, I give my engaged clients and married clients this assignment. I ask them to write down all the things they like about their spouse or intended spouse. With married people, I limit them to five things because for some reason, by the time married people come for counseling, they struggle to find five things about each other that they like.

And the reason for that is found in a coin. Look at a coin. What do you see? You see the head. We usually identify the head with the winning decision. It's the strong side. You will also see the tail. The tail we associate with losing, wrong choices, and weakness. But few of us ever say, "I see the edge". And yet the coin is what it is because there is a head, a tail and an edge that holds it together.

Human personality is like a coin. Oftentimes after we get physical attractiveness out of the way, we get to like a person because of their strengths. Usually, we are attracted to those strengths that we lack in ourselves. Thus, the overly serious woman falls in love with a man who makes her laugh. When he is around, she feels light-hearted and so very happy. They get married. She laughs the first day, the first week, and the first month. Until something *serious* takes place and he still finds it funny.

By the time, they come to me. It's a major problem. The wife complains, "Everything is funny to him, he never takes things seriously." The husband complains, "My wife has no sense of humor, I really wish she would lighten up. She used to always laugh at my jokes, now I can't get her to crack a smile".

What has happened? The husband's strength, his wonderful sense of humor, his ability to see and help others to enjoy the lighter side of life, is the head. But it is connected to a weakness that was overlooked during the "honeymoon" phase of the relationship. This weakness can manifest as poor planning, lack of ambition and personal drive or just simply as inappropriate responses to serious situations. It does not matter how the other side of the coin manifests itself, it results in a lose/lose situation for the person at the end of the criticism. He or she begins to feel "I can never win".

I can go on to give you hundreds of examples of how this plays out in relationships.

"He is so hardworking"	*"He is a workaholic"*
"She is disciplined in spending"	*"She is a tightwad and so controlling"*
"He is such a generous person"	*"He has no business sense, he is so gullible"*
"She is a great planner"	*"She is not spontaneous"*

I hope you've gotten the picture. For every strength, there is a weakness that manifests itself and may irritate, disappoint, or even hurt you. But it's what makes what you love about the person, loveable.

I'm not saying that destructive behavior is acceptable. But I am saying that we must learn to concentrate and applaud and admire our spouses' strengths and minimize their weaknesses, because whatever we give attention to is going to grow larger and larger in our eyes.

While I am on this topic, I need to also address our "weaknesses".

In premarital counseling, I ask couples to list five weaknesses or things that they do not like about the person they are planning to marry. Oh, how they sometimes struggle, because they are SO in love that they see everything through rose-colored glasses. But after much prompting, I am usually able to get something out of them. Some very sheepishly admit what they see as a fault in the other person. Others are very bold and forthright about what they have written.

The next question I ask is, "Can you live with this for the rest of your life?" I know that it shocks them. I am always intentional about shocking them. I want them to know that they may get what they want but they may eventually not want what they get.

Too many couples enter a marriage relationship with the hope that marriage will change their partner, only to end up in the divorce courts because the other person never changed but in fact grew worse.

My husband always makes a very wise statement about money. He says, "Money does not change a person, it simply magnifies who they are". If they were generous before they had a lot of money, they will be more generous when they have more. If they were selfish before, they will be more selfish with more money.

The same is true for marriage. Characteristics that you see in a person before you marry, qualities that you do not like, will be magnified under the microscope of marriage.

Do not marry a person thinking that you are going to change him or her. In my first book, "A Woman and Her Pastor", I identified, *The Changer*. This kind of woman, I said, is attracted to men who have serious character flaws. She gets into relationships with them because she somehow sees herself as the one person who will be able to change them. It's as though she has a need to believe that she is needed and that she is appointed and assigned to be this man's savior. Too late she finds out that no one can change another person who does not see the need to change and does not have the desire to change.

I am not saying that people cannot change. I am however saying, that it is only the Holy Spirit who can bring about lasting change in an individual's life. Even so, change only happens, when that individual cooperates with the Holy Spirit.

When a husband or a wife sets himself or herself up in the place of the Holy Spirit to bring about change in the spouse, it results in frustration on both sides and can eventually lead to separation and divorce.

It never ceases to amaze me that people, men and women alike, will walk into a marriage with both eyes open and deliberately reason away serious character flaws in the other person. They say to me that it's just one thing. Now if the "one thing" is a simple thing such as leaving the toilet seat up or down, or squeezing the tube of toothpaste from the top, middle or bottom, I would say overlook it. But when the person you are thinking of marrying is extremely controlling and domineering or extremely jealous; when that person belittles you, is disrespectful to the people you admire and respect, often flies into an uncontrollable rage, is violent, makes threats to you and those you love, my recommendation is RUN FOR YOUR LIFE AND DON'T LOOK BACK. DO NOT PASS GO. DO NOT COLLECT $200. DO NOT MARRY THIS PERSON. YOU ARE SETTING UP YOURSELF TO BE A STATISTIC.

However, please know that even if your fiancé does not display any serious negative behaviors, because no one is perfect, including you, there are behaviors that will come with him or her that you must decide about. This is the decision you must make. Are you committed to live in unconditional love with your spouse, taking into consideration those characteristics that are not so lovely? If your answer is no, DO NOT MARRY and then nag your spouse later about something you saw but did not confront because you were desperate. I'm just telling it like it is and I'm not pulling any punches. My job is not to flatter you, or to justify you in your foolishness but to save you and your yet unborn children from a miserable life. Remember we started this discourse on the premise that marriage is not just about us. Our marriages reflect Christ and His Bride, the Church.

Romans 15: 1- 6 in the Weymouth New Testament reads like this:

> *As for us who are strong, our duty is to bear with the weaknesses of those who are not strong, and not seek our own pleasure. Let each of us endeavor to please his fellow Christian, aiming at a blessing calculated to build him up. For even the Christ did not seek His own pleasure. His principle was, "The reproaches which they addressed to Thee have fallen on me." For all that was written of old has been written for our instruction, so that we may always have hope through the power of endurance and the encouragement which the*

Scriptures afford. And may God, the giver of power of endurance and of that encouragement, grant you to be in full sympathy with one another in accordance with the example of Christ Jesus, 6so that with oneness both of heart and voice you may glorify the God and Father of our Lord Jesus Christ.

This scripture was really written in the context of the controversies that had arisen in the early church as it related to matter of the law and the different behaviors of the Jewish and Gentile Christians. But how relevant it is for relationships in general, particularly the marriage relationship. We must "bear each other's weaknesses and not seek our own pleasure". We must endeavor to please each other and be intentional in building up one another. Other translations speak of being "patient" with each other's weaknesses.

Married people need to go back and remember what they saw in their mates that attracted them in the first place and caused them to love them. Whatever that thing was, needs to be kept before you daily and admired. Stop looking at the grass on the other side. It may appear greener but that may be because there's a whole lot more "poop" over there.

Start appreciating the person you have. It may be that your husband is not one who fixes stuff around the house, but if he cooks for you, or comes straight home from work and watches television with you, there are hundreds of women who would line up at the door if you were giving him away. Your wife may not seem to be all that exciting, but if she always has your back, believes, and supports your ideas, manages the finances so that the creditors are not calling, there are a hundred of men who will line up at the door if you were giving her away.

Percy Sledge said it best in the lyric of this old song, "if you think nobody else wants your man (or woman) just kick them out and throw them in the street, someone will have him (her) before you can count "one, two, three".

This then is the conclusion of the matter. Everyone has a head, and a tail but the edge that must hold it together is our unconditional love for each other.

REVIEW

1. *List 5 of your weaknesses that you need your spouse to be patient with.*

   _____

   _____

   _____

   _____

   _____

2. *List 2 of your spouse or intended spouse's strengths.*

   _____

   _____

3. *In what way, might or do these strengths manifest as weaknesses?*

   _____

   _____

   _____

4. *How do you intend to "bear" or be patient with these weaknesses?*

   _____

   _____

   _____

"We also must do all that is within our power to live at peace with each other's family members."

FAMILY MATTERS

A couple drove down a country road for several miles, not saying a word. An earlier discussion had led to an argument and neither of them wanted to concede their position. As they passed a barnyard of mules, goats and pigs, the husband asked sarcastically, "Relatives of yours?" "Yep," the wife replied, "in-laws."

"What God has joined together, let no man, no woman, no in-law, no outlaw put asunder". This is the humorous version of the marriage vow that my husband usually uses after he pronounces a couple, husband and wife.

Some people say that they don't really care how their

spouse's family relate to them because they married their spouse, not his or her family. But there are also others who decide not to marry someone because of that person's family.

We can't deny the fact that family can have a huge influence on a couple's marriage one way or another. Some families intervene to prevent a marriage from taking place. I recently heard a story about a bride who was left standing at the altar because the groom's family apparently drugged him so that he would not attend his wedding. They did not approve of the girl he was going to marry and were determined that by any means necessary, she would not become his wife.

William's Shakespeare's tragedy "Romeo and Juliet" was based upon two lovers whose families were feuding against each other. A failed attempt to be with each other, resulted in a double suicide. The families were reconciled, but at a great cost, the death of their children.

On the island where I was born, I heard modern day Romeo and Juliet stories of young people kept apart from each other because of religious differences or status differences or racial differences, who resorted to suicide rather than live without each other.

As a young sixteen- year- old myself, I started dating a young man of a different race, and while my parents were very open to him, his family would have none of it. Racial division was so bad in my island that when he became ill with pneumonia, I could not visit him at his home. He came out to the front porch of his home so that I could speak with him from the street outside.

Scenarios like this continue to be played out repeatedly in every generation. It is only the very strong who can hold their marriages together despite disapproving, and in some cases, hostile family members.

Even Moses experienced this kind of hostility from his older brother and sister, Aaron, and Miriam.

Numbers 12:1 Miriam and Aaron spoke against Moses because of the Cushite woman whom he had married, for he had married a Cushite woman.

They were so upset with Moses' choice of a wife that it led them to more negative speech against Moses which brought God's anger down on them and judgement upon Miriam. This should warn us that we should be very careful about interfering in the relationship between husbands and wives, even if they are family.

Does family matter? How much consideration should be given to the other person's relatives in deciding to marry? Are we really marrying INTO the other person's family or not?

Whenever I am confronted with questions like these, I always put myself on the side of the Word of God because that is the only true rule we can use as a measurement. Let me reiterate what I said at the beginning of this book, it's not about us. God made marriage the foremost earthly institution. In the book of beginnings, it is recorded:

> ***Genesis 2:23-24 The man said, "This is now bone of my bones, And flesh of my flesh; She shall be called Woman, Because she was taken out of Man." For this reason a man shall leave his father and his mother, and be joined to his wife; and they shall become one flesh.***

This command to leave the closest family relationship (that of one's father and mother) and to cleave (stick to, or adhere to) one's wife, is repeated several times in the New Testament.

> ***Matthew 19:5***
> ***…. 'For this reason a man will leave his father and mother and be united to his wife, and the two will become one flesh'***

> ***Mark 10:7***
> ***For this reason a man will leave his father and mother and be united to his wife,***
> ***Mark 10:8***
> ***and the two will become one flesh.' So, they are no longer two, but one flesh.***

1 Corinthians 6:16

Do you not know that he who unites himself with a prostitute is one with her in body? For it is said, "The two will become one flesh."

Ephesians 5:31

"For this reason a man will leave his father and mother and be united to his wife, and the two will become one flesh."

In the context of the Bible, "leaving father and mother" is not only geographical, but also financial and emotional. Family, especially extended family members, should not be allowed to interfere in the relationship between husband and wife. Of course, I am not saying that where there is abuse, neglect, and other unbiblical practices, that family members should just turn a blind eye. There are situations in which intervention is necessary to prevent harm coming to one of the parties.

However, courting couples need to face the reality that if they are from different family backgrounds and different cultures, or different religions, their differences, and their expectations need to be openly and honestly discussed with each other before they decide to marry. Love alone, that is, the emotional aspect of love, does not necessarily cause these differences to be acceptable once the union has taken place.

Couples should discuss before marriage what role if any, each other's family is going to play in this new family that they are starting. What about family reunions? What about significant holidays? Do we spend it at your family or my family? What if I want to go and you don't? Should the need arise to take in an aging or widowed parent, what will we do? How much financial support will we give to our parents if it becomes necessary?

Husbands and wives must agree that a shift must now take place and that their primary human relationship is no longer their parents or parental figure, their siblings or even the children that they have or will have, but each other. This is a hard saying but it is fundamental to a healthy marriage relationship. When either the man or the woman allows family members or friends to become involved in the decision-making processes of their marriage, it is only a matter of time before this new "ship" will flounder on the rocks of well-intentioned and not-so-well-intentioned interference from outside parties.

What is even worse is that oftentimes, those outside parties are either not married themselves or have major problems in their marriages, yet want to offer counsel to the new couple.

To sum it up, family matters. But the couple has to agree to what degree each other's family is going to matter. There must be a commitment to each other that will supersede the commitment to the former families. The husband must be able to stand up for his wife if his mother or any other female relative is attempting to devalue her and the wife needs to defend her husband likewise.

We also must do all that is within our power to live at peace with each other's family members. While no one expects that we must become people pleasers, God expects us to be peace makers.

> ***Hebrews 12:14-15 (NIV) Make every effort to live in peace with everyone and to be holy; without holiness, no one will see the Lord. See to it that no one falls short of the grace of God and that no bitter root grows up to cause trouble and defile many***

God wants us to exert energy in living in peace with everyone including our spouse's family members. He also expects us to guard against having bitterness, resentment, and anger against everyone, including in-laws.

REVIEW

1. *What is the primary human relationship in any couple's marriage?*

   _____
   _____
   _____

2. *What kind of discussions about their respective families should every couple have before they marry?*

   _____
   _____
   _____
   _____

3. *What is involved in "leaving" father and mother?*

   _____
   _____
   _____

4. *What is our responsibility in living peacefully with our in-laws?*

   _____
   _____
   _____

"Financial wisdom does not necessarily come naturally. But it is imperative that we acquire it."

chapter 07

MONEY MATTERS TOO

SON: "Daddy, how much does it cost to get married?"
FATHER: "I don't know, son, I'm still paying for it."

I don't know whether you realize that many marriages fall apart not because of infidelity but because of money.

Unfortunately, a lot of couples do not discuss money matters while they are dating or courting because, to them, it is not important. And even if one partner may want to broach the subject, he or she may not want to come across as being "money-minded".

However, disagreements about whose money is it, how money should or should not be spent, who is responsible for paying bills, and so on, cause couples to end up in the divorce court more often than you would care to imagine. It is therefore vital that couples discuss these issues and come to an agreement before they marry or, if already married, take the time, and have an open discussion about this important topic.

WHOSE MONEY IS IT?

Couples need to decide whose money is it. Is it my money? Is it your money? Or is it our money?

We have very complex issues today because of so many different models of money management in marriage. Long ago the model was that the husband was the bread winner and the wife was the home maker. This model was a simple model and could be considered the original model which still exists in some families today. In this model however, there is opportunity for disagreement. Does the husband bring all the money home to the wife and give her free rein on managing the money? Is the wife even allowed to know how much money her husband earns? Does he take care of all the bills and dole out to her what he feels is needed for groceries and other necessities? What if she wants to help her parents financially? Is the wife required to request from her husband every dollar she wants or needs?

I once heard the story of a woman who had established a very successful jewelry business. Someone asked her what motivated her to start and build such a successful business. To which she responded that one day she asked her husband for ten dollars. He in turn asked her, "what for?" She said that was the moment she decided that she would never ask him for any money ever again. It drove her to build her own successful business.

The most common model today is one in which both husband and wife work. Some couples see it as the only way to meet all their financial obligations. However, additional income leads to other issues, such as more taxes, competition between spouses, and emotional stress.

Over the last thirty years or so, we began to see another model emerge. In this model, the husband stays at home and the wife goes out to work. There are many reasons why some couples find this model works better for them. Sometimes, the wife's job pays her so much more than her husband's job and child care services are so expensive, that the couple makes a financial decision that the man should stay at home with their children while the wife continues at her job. In some cases, this arrangement is temporary so that the husband can go back to college to become more employable.

Whichever model you choose, the same issues arise. Whose money is it anyway? Who should make the decisions as to how the money is to be spent? Do we have joint bank accounts and joint credit cards? Should either spouse get involved in a debt without consulting with the other person? What about student loans and credit card debt that are being brought into the marriage? Who is responsible for paying them? Should either spouse have a secret account? Do I have to consult my spouse on every purchase that I make?

Money matters become more complex as state law and federal law must be considered. In the state of Florida, for instance, a woman cannot purchase a home without including her husband's name on the mortgage. Consequently, even if the woman is the principal bread winner and the principal person paying for the home, the property is nonetheless as much her husband's as it is hers.

Child support concerns also lead to serious complications in marriages. There are so many stories of women marrying men who have children with another woman, only to find out that their two salaries cannot support their new union because his income is an "outcome". It never comes in because almost his entire salary is being garnished for child support. Couples who have issues like this should seek legal and financial counsel before they marry. If not, the financial burdens that they encounter can lead to so much friction that the stability of their marriage is severely challenged.

TO GIVE OR NOT TO GIVE

Giving is also an aspect of money that can be a source of conflict. Couples can have strong disagreement as to how much money should be allotted to tithes and offerings or other charitable giving.

When family members fall on hard times and reach out for help, it can be a source of contention as to whether to lend, to give or to do neither.

We can see that it is essential that financial planning be a part of pre-marital counseling. Couples who did not do this should seek advice from a professional adviser early in their marriage to avoid the pitfalls or resentment and bitterness that these issues can lead to.

What is the biblical approach to all of this? Solomon says it well:

*"Wisdom is of utmost importance, therefore get wisdom,
and with all your effort work to acquire understanding.
Proverbs 4:7*

Your upbringing has a lot to do with how you view money, spend money or conserve money. So, unless you were raised in a home where your parents were very proficient in handling money, it is unlikely that you have the skills necessary to handle some of the complexities. Financial wisdom does not necessarily come naturally. But it is imperative that we acquire it.

Money can bring out the best in us, but it can also bring out the worst in us. My husband always says that money does not change people, it simply magnifies who they are.

Consequently, when it involves money, a couple will do well to apply the principles of 1 Corinthians 13: 4-8 - *Love is patient, love is kind. It does not envy, it does not boast, it is not proud. It does not dishonor others, it is not self-seeking, it is not easily angered, it keeps no record of wrongs. Love does not delight in evil but rejoices with the truth. It always protects, always trusts, always hopes, always perseveres. (NIV)*

GOD SAYS IT'S HIS

It is also important to have a biblical perspective concerning stewardship. When the Christian couple is committed to biblical problem solving, they begin to understand that the material possessions they have is neither "his", "hers" or "theirs", but "HIS", that is, God's. Everything we possess truly belongs to God. He only gives us the privilege of being responsible stewards of all that He grants us.

Eccl. 5:15 Everyone comes naked from their mother's womb, and as everyone comes, so they depart. They take nothing from their toil that they can carry in their hands.

Psalm 49:17 For when he dies he will carry nothing away; His glory will not descend after him.

1 Timothy 6:7 After all, we brought nothing with us when we came into the world, and we can't take anything with us when we leave it. (New Living Translation)

Since everything we possess truly belongs to God, where is there room for a husband and wife to argue over money? There is no room. Both parties, being committed to biblical problem solving, should therefore consult the Lord together and seek His will as it relates to decisions on spending, saving, investing and giving.

We are accountable to God. We are also accountable to each other. When we realize that it is God who gives us the power to get wealth (Deuteronomy 8:18), we develop a new perspective on giving to others and helping those who are in a less fortunate position than we are. We put away childish behavior and operate with the God kind of love that never fails.

I used to believe that the correct "married" behavior was to have joint accounts for everything, including credit cards. It was only when my husband and I wanted to buy our first home, that I discovered that joint debt was not always a good idea. Consequently, he had to remove my name from some credit cards so that we could qualify for a mortgage.

I also discovered later in our marriage that I was not the better person to handle our finances. I was making more money than my husband at the time because I had a government job and the salary he got from the church was not enough to take care of our financial responsibilities. He had his account and added my name. I had my account and added his name. But I was always in the red with my account. I remember very clearly the day the Lord ministered to me to bring my salary under the leadership of my husband and to let him manage our money. It was the most liberating thing, I ever did! A burden was rolled away! My husband made certain that the bills were paid on time and as the years passed, our financial positions changed to the point that "my" money was really "my" pocket change to spend as I pleased.

Now before you men rush ahead and demand that your wives do the same, you should know that I felt secure in such a move because my husband had already demonstrated three essential characteristics:

a. *He saw me as an equal partner from whom he hid nothing and with whom he consulted before making decisions.*
b. *He had already demonstrated that he was responsible with saving money and paying bills.*
c. *He was not "stingy" nor selfish. It was, and still is, his great motivation, to provide a lifestyle for his family, that far surpasses what he experienced growing up.*

Every couple must know who is more proficient and efficient in handling their finances and allow that person, whether it is the husband or the wife to do so. But at the same time, whoever has that privilege must understand that the other person is not their child, nor their subordinate and that he or she should always treat their spouse with respect and with consideration, recognizing him or her as an equal partner.

REVIEW

1. *List some of the questions you want to ask your fiancé or you wish you had asked your spouse before getting married.*

   _____
   _____
   _____

2. *Which of the three models described, best depict your marriage and what are some of the challenges you are experiencing?*

   _____
   _____
   _____

3. *What were your parents' views on Spending? Saving? Investing? Giving?*

   _____
   _____
   _____

4. *What biblical perspective about material possessions should govern our actions concerning money?*

   _____
   _____
   _____

"Any successful establishment has someone who is recognized as the head of that company. God, in His wisdom has ordained that in the marriage relationship, there is a head..."

chapter 08

WHO'S THE BOSS

Marriage is when a man and woman become as one; the trouble starts when they try to decide which one.

One of my favorite television shows when I was growing up was "Who's the Boss? It was a comedy featuring a busy female executive and her housekeeper, who was a handsome, Italian man.

"You may be the head but I'm the neck", many women have jokingly said. The question of headship in marriage is a subject that is debated in our time more than ever before.

Changes in society, especially in our Western culture, have caused a feeling of ambivalence as to who is the head of the home. Even in the Christian church, the lines of demarcation have become faded as more women have taken up positions of leadership there.

It's a very fine line that we as women must walk today. There is so much that we want to do, while at the same time we don't want to run ahead of our husbands. It becomes even more difficult when the husband in question is very passive or laid back and the wife is an enterprising person who wants to see things happen for her family.

BORN TO RULE

Often, women don't know how to handle this constant struggle between following and leading. What is the right thing to do? If my husband is not doing anything about our situation should I sit back and just let the ship sink because he is the captain?

These are difficult questions to answer but it helps when we understand that the ability to lead was deposited in both the man and the woman.

Genesis 1:28 (NIV)
God blessed them and said to them, "Be fruitful and increase in

number; fill the earth and subdue it. Rule over the fish in the sea and the birds in the sky and over every living creature that moves on the ground."

Look at the words "subdue" and "rule". They imply dominion, headship, and leadership. Adam and Eve, the first married couple, were given equal sovereignty over the earth. This means that inherent in the woman as well as the man is the ability and even the desire to be the boss. But something changed everything on the part of the woman.

After the Fall, God established a new order. In fact, He handed down a judgement on the woman because she had taken the lead and flagrantly disobeyed God's command and had also involved her husband in the transgression.

Genesis 3:6 KJV
And when the woman saw that the tree was good for food, and that it was pleasant to the eyes, and a tree to be desired to make one wise, she took of the fruit thereof, and did eat, and gave also unto her husband with her; and he did eat.

God tells the woman that because of her actions, He was instituting a change of status. Her husband would now become her manager and would rule over her.

Genesis 3:16 KJV
Unto the woman he said, I will greatly multiply thy sorrow and

thy conception; in sorrow, thou shalt bring forth children; and thy desire shall be to thy husband, and he shall rule over thee

The New Testament restates this relationship in **1 Corinthians 11:3**

But I want you to understand that the head of every man is Christ, the head of a wife is her husband, and the head of Christ is God. ESV

Ephesians 5:22 NIV
Wives, submit yourselves to your own husbands as you do to the Lord. 23For the husband is the head of the wife as Christ is the head of the church, his body, of which he is the Savior. 24Now as the church submits to Christ, so also wives should submit to their husbands in everything.

The word "submission" evokes very strong emotions in most women. Partly because men and church leaders have badgered women over the head with it for centuries, totally ignoring verse 21 which encourages all of us to "submit to one another". I am so grateful for the Amplified Bible which helped me to have a proper understanding of what it means to submit.

Some of the key concepts that I have taken from this version are the concepts of admiration, respect and deference or yielding. I have discovered that most husbands crave admiration from their wives. Unfortunately, too many of us fail to give it because we focus on what our husbands fail to do instead of what our husbands successfully do. One of my emphases in marriage counseling is to seek to get women to understand that it is impossible to find every quality that you desire in your husband. And that instead of finding fault with him, wives need to appreciate every positive quality that there is in their husbands because many other women would be happy to have the kind of husband you have.

Men also need respect. It amazes me sometimes that so many women are unable to give their husbands the same respect that they give to their male bosses at work. At home, the same woman who may have respectfully made her boss a cup of coffee, refuses to serve her husband.

The Amplified Bible also speaks about deferring and yielding to one's husband. I have found my best illustration of this in the road sign. As drivers, we know that we must give way to the other motorist if the yield sign is on our side. Similarly, in the marriage relationship, if couples cannot come to an agreement in a matter, the yield sign is on the woman's side. Now this does not mean that the husband is always right or that he will always make the right decision. But in God's system of order, he has the right to be wrong.

Those of us who have participated in sports, know that the coach does not always make the right call, but because we understand team spirit, we do not upbraid the coach for making a bad call. Our responsibility as Christian wives, is to pray fervently for our husbands so that they can hear from Christ who is their head. Then they will lead us in the right way.

I know that I have not addressed other issues such as abusive husbands, lazy husbands, weak husbands and so on. Although, it's not within the scope of this book to deal with all of this, I cannot move on without letting you know that in no way does God countenance ungodly behavior by husbands. In fact, He instructs believers in general, how we ought to treat one another, and tells husbands, how to treat their wives so that they can have their prayers answered.

> *1 Peter 3: 7 – 9 AMP*
>
> *In the same way, you husbands, live with your wives in an understanding way [with great gentleness and tact, and with an intelligent regard for the marriage relationship], as with someone physically weaker, since she is a woman. Show her honor and respect as a fellow heir of the grace of life, so that your prayers will not be hindered or ineffective.*
>
> *8 Finally, all of you be like-minded [united in spirit], sympathetic, brotherly, kindhearted [courteous and compassionate toward each other as members of one*

household], and humble in spirit; 9 and never return evil for evil or insult for insult [avoid scolding, berating, and any kind of abuse], but on the contrary, give a blessing [pray for one another's well-being, contentment, and protection]; for you have been called for this very purpose, that you might inherit a blessing [from God that brings well-being, happiness, and protection]

In no way does the Bible imply that women are inferior to men. Peter, in advising the wife of the unbelieving husband how to relate to her husband in a biblical way, is careful to point out that by choosing to be subordinate does not mean that she is inferior.

1 Peter 3:1 (AMP)
In the same way, you wives, be [a]submissive to your own husbands [subordinate, not as inferior, but out of respect for the responsibilities entrusted to husbands and their accountability to God, and so partnering with them] so that even if some do not obey the word [of God], they may be won over [to Christ] without discussion by the godly lives of their wives

Any successful establishment has someone who is recognized as the head of that company. God, in His wisdom has ordained that in the marriage relationship, there is a head and that head is the man, not the woman. The husband's headship is a serious God-given responsibility, for which God will hold men accountable. Therefore, men, it is imperative that you properly understand headship. If you misunderstand the concept of headship you will not be able to properly fulfil your role as head of your wife.

WHAT HEADSHIP IS NOT

Headship is not control. I get scared for women who get into relationships with men who want to control them. The spirit of control is a Jezebel spirit. It manifests itself as unreasonable jealousy. This type of man does not want his wife to speak to or be spoken to by other men. Sometimes he is even jealous of her relationship with her female friends and her family. He gradually cuts her off from all other important relationships in her life. Sometimes this control manifests itself by withholding money or information about the finances of the family.

Headship is not dictatorship. Because you are the head does not mean that your wife cannot have an opinion, does not have a voice, and does not have a valuable contribution to make. In fact, she is your helper, and God has given her insight that can serve to protect you many times from making mistakes that you might regret.

Headship is not superiority. It does not mean that because

you are the head that you are necessarily, wiser, smarter, stronger, or better.

It DOES mean that you get the opportunity to be a servant-leader. Jesus, the Head of the Church, said that if He as Lord and Master served His disciples, we should follow His example.

WHAT HEADSHIP IS

Headship, at its lowest level or definition is a call. God has called you, the husband to be the head of your wife and family. Now it's up to you to define and refine your headship and leadership style within that call.

Are you going to be the type of leader that your wife follows only because you constantly remind her that you are the man in the house? Then your headship will not go beyond the positional level, which is the second level.

At the third level, your wife and family will follow you because they want to. They will submit to you because they love and trust you. Any husband who consistently "nourishes" and "cherishes" his wife, and loves her as his own body will experience the honor of having voluntary submission from his wife. His wife will adapt herself to him.

As the head of your home, your headship or leadership will ascend to a higher level when your family sees the results of your leadership not just in your life, but also in their own lives, as a by-product of your leadership.

And last of all, the highest level of headship is seen when you raise up leaders in your home. As the head of your wife, has she been able to achieve her highest potential? Have you surrounded her with an environment where she has felt safe to cultivate her talents and gifts? Have those talents and gifts remained dormant or even died because you felt threatened that she was better in certain areas than you were? Psalms 128:3 describes the man who has achieved this level of leadership "your wife will be like a fruitful vine within your house; your children will be like olive shoots around your table."

Solomon asks in Proverbs 31 "who can find a virtuous woman?". He goes on to describe this phenomenal woman who buys property, takes care of her household, is industrious, does her husband good and displays a host of other qualities that cause her husband to praise her. But in a day when most women were relegated to a subservient position, this woman's husband had to have been a remarkable man and leader to have allowed his wife to be all that she could be.

So, who's the boss? Biblically speaking, the husband is. But with that position comes a tremendous responsibility to fulfil what God requires of the man in his role as head of his wife and family, and as a representative of Christ.

A man who understands his true role helps his wife to become all that she was meant to be. He is not in competition with her. He does not feel intimidated or threatened by her success.

The woman who understands headship and graciously yields to her husband, helps him to become the man that God intended him to be. She, in turn, benefits from the joy of knowing that there is someone else who can shoulder the burdens that God never intended her to carry.

REVIEW:

1. *What are some of the words that are synonymous with "submit"?*

   _____

2. *What three behaviors are not equivalent to headship?*

   _____

   _____

   _____

3. *Name the 5 levels of headship.*

   _____

   _____

   _____

   _____

   _____

4. *(For husbands) In what area do you see yourself improving as the head of your wife?*

   _____

   _____

5. *(For wives) How can you improve in showing respect to your husband?*

   _____

   _____

"...most people know that we should put God first, but miss it on the second priority..."

chapter 09

WHO'S FIRST?

Sometimes you cannot tell if a man is trying so hard to be a success to please his wife or to spite his mother-in-law.

I remember as a young person being confronted with this hypothetical scenario. You are in a life and death situation. You can save only one person. Who will you choose, your mother, your spouse, or your child?

People disagree on the answer to this question, but society generally agrees on the concept of women and children first.

However, most people do not realize that as it relates to family relationships there is a biblical order of priorities.

To find out where my counselees stand on this, I usually give them a list in no prioritized order. I then ask them to arrange it according to what the order is in their lives. Then I have them rearrange it according to what they believe the order ought to be. Here is that list. Go to the review section and do the first assignment before continuing to read.

SPOUSE, JOB, GOD, CHURCH, CHILDREN, SOCIETY

How did you do? Who or what has first, second, third, fourth and fifth place in your life.

I hope that God is first. And by that I do not mean that you know in your head that He should have that place. I mean that very consciously and intentionally you give Him priority in your life. Do you make decisions based on what you believe is His plan and will for your life? Do you even consult Him when opportunities present themselves for job promotion, business investments, moving from one location to another? Does He take priority over everything else in your life or is He just an afterthought with you?

God wants to have the first place in our lives. He wants it not for His sake but for ours. The Bible is full of admonitions to put

Him first. When God established relationship with the Israelites, He commanded them to "Love the Lord your God with all your soul, all your mind and all your heart."

Jesus reiterated the preeminence of God's position. When the rich, young ruler asked Him, which was the first and greatest commandment, without a pause, Jesus answered him, **"Love the Lord your God with all your soul, all your might and all your strength." (Matthew 22:36-40)**

Solomon, acclaimed by all to be the wisest, natural man who ever walked on this earth, advised us to **"acknowledge Him in all your ways and He will direct your paths". (Proverbs 3:6)**

Doesn't it just make sense to hook up with the One who knows all, sees all and can do all things?

> *Jeremiah 29:11*
> *For I know the plans I have for you," declares the Lord, "plans to prosper you and not to harm you, plans to give you hope and a future?*

Paul, the apostle summed it up in this way, **"Eye has not seen, neither has ear heard, neither has it entered into the heart of man, the things that God has prepared for those who love Him (1 Corinthians 2:9).** If this does not get you excited, I don't know what will. But every time I meditate on this, it inspires me.

The wonderful thing is that we don't have to wonder if He's serious. He's dead serious. I mean that. He did not spare His Own Son but delivered Him up freely for us all. You must deal with the historical Jesus even if you say you don't believe in God. If He was just a zealot on a mission that was aborted by His death, how do you account for the fact that today, despite all the efforts to annihilate the memory of Him, His teachings, and His people, He is still the foremost person who ever lived?

Now most people know that we should put God first, but miss it on the second priority, their spouse. You will be surprised how many well-intentioned Christians believe that church should have second place in their lives. They may not say, but they act it out. But after God, it is your spouse that must have priority.

Jesus, in answer to the rich, young ruler said, "and the second commandment is like the first, you shall love your neighbor as yourself". Then he went on to explain who our neighbor is, by telling the story of the good Samaritan who put the comfort and well-being of the person in need above his own comfort, needs and well-being.

But who is your closest neighbor if not your spouse? Your spouse is so close to you that God sees you as one. "The two shall become one flesh". The apostle, Paul, elaborated on this concept by telling husbands that they must love their wives as their own bodies. (Ephesians 5:28) He said no man ever hated his body but nourishes and cherishes it. Therefore, he admonished husbands to love their wives and to demonstrate it by cherishing them.

A woman feels nourished and cherished when she is first in her husband's affections, when he considers her feelings and does not make light of her opinions. She does not want to compete with his mother's cooking or with the way her neighbors keep their houses. And she does not want to be in competition with his job, the guys or another woman for his time.

The wife too, must love her husband. Paul told Pastor Titus, to have the older women teach the younger women how to love their husbands. (Titus 2:4) This is something to ponder over. If love just comes naturally, how is it that older women can teach younger women to love their husbands?

If you want to be successful in marriage, seek out a God-fearing Christian woman who has remained married to the same man for twenty years or more. I guarantee you that she has a lot of wise advice as to what to do and what not to do in certain situations. She has come into some understanding of the psyche of men in general and of her own husband. She has come to understand that her husband does not want to compete with another man, the children, her job, the housework, her friends and even her pastimes.

Third, in the order of priorities, are your children. Yes, they are not first nor second. This priority gets confused during those first few years of their lives, when these demanding beings are dependent on parents for their very lives. We feed them, change them, when they have messed on themselves, and comfort them when they cannot communicate what their discomfort is. Unfortunately, old habits die hard and young couples continue to prioritize the needs of their children above everything else. Consequently, the couple builds their lives on the foundation of their children. They desire the best for their children and so their decisions to move or not to move, to buy or not to buy, to invest or not to invest are tied to their children. They stop going on dates. They never go on a vacation without their children. In some extreme cases, they stop making love on a regular basis. All because of the children. More dangerously, one or the other parent, sometimes takes the side of the children over their spouse. The relationship degenerates, but the children are the glue that keeps their parents together.

In other cases, the relationship appears fine on the outside and there is no obvious hostility between the parents. However, once the nest becomes empty and the last child has left to build his own life, the parents have a dilemma. They do not know how to relate to each other now that the children have left. All their decisions, conversation and energy revolved around the children and they failed to continue to cultivate their own relationship and to strengthen the bond between them. They failed to understand that their children "came to go" but their spouse "came to stay until death would part them". Sadly, we hear of these marriages falling apart after twenty or more years of marriage.

Next in the order of priorities, should be the church. Through the church, your service to God finds expression. Christ loved the Church and gave Himself for her. The Church is His Body and therefore we should seek to demonstrate and show our love to Him by loving whom He loves. It's not God's will that your responsibilities at church take pre-eminence over your responsibilities to your spouse or your children. Pastors often have the most difficult time separating the two. This may account for the fact that so many pastors' kids become statistics along the way because these children grew up their entire lives as emotional orphans. The church always won. They grew up feeling neglected and unloved by their parents. They felt resentful towards the church that took their parents from them.

Your job, occupation or business comes next because this is vehicle God has given you to take care of spouse, children, and church. It's very easy to fall into the trap of getting into the vehicle and leaving the passengers behind. But it is important to realize that our source is God and that our job, or business is a resource that He continually replenishes. A resource can dry up but once we are connected to the Source, another resource will always open again.

Elijah got accustomed to the ravens bringing him food and the brook giving him water, but when the ravens seemed to have lost his address and the brook dried up, God told him to go to Zarephath because He had another unlikely candidate, He had commanded a widow to feed him there.

If we come to a place where our job takes priority, we cannot hear from God. When the business fails or our job is downsized, or our health makes it difficult to continue with our career, we come to the sad realization that we gained the whole world, but in the process, we lost our relationship with God, our spouse, our children, and the Church.

The next time you are offered a job or a promotion, the first question to ask yourself is "how is this going to affect my primary relationships?" The prestige may be more and the material benefits may be better, but if it's going to seriously impinge on the time that you must consecrate to God, family, and church, you must seriously question whether you are hearing from God concerning the decision you are about to make.

Last in order of priority is our social life constituting of friends, other relationships, civic involvement, and pastimes.

None of these should take the place of any of the others already mentioned. You would think that we should know this without someone having to tell us. But how many times have we heard the story of the wife who feels left behind in the wake of her husband's love for a sport, or who feels devalued in the presence of his friends? And what about the husband who feels that his wife gives preference to her relatives over him or leaves him and their children behind in the wake of her passion for her career?

Let's take an honest look at our lives. Where are our priorities? We must honestly answer this question because whenever any one of these priorities is out of order, we have disorder. Our marriage cannot thrive in an atmosphere of disorder. God is not the author of confusion. He cannot bring His best to pass until He corrects chaos. I recently read this *"You cannot prosper in all things when you overlook aspects of your life that create chaos and result in destruction." (Marsha Burns, <u>Small Straws in a Soft Wind</u>, March 24, 2017)*

If we go back to the beginning in Genesis 1: 1- 3 we see the earth in a state of chaos, without form, empty, dark and God said "Let there be light". Allow the same Spirit of God that moved upon the face of the waters, to move upon you today and bring His light into your situation so that you can have His best. You can hear His pronouncement that what He sees is good.

REVIEW:

1. *Arrange the following list in order of their priority in your life: SPOUSE, JOB, GOD, CHURCH, CHILDREN, SOCIETY*

   _____

   _____

   _____

2. *Arrange the same list in what you believe is the biblical priority.*

   _____

   _____

   _____

3. *Reference one Bible verse that admonishes us to put God first.*

   _____

   _____

   _____

   _____

4. *Reference one Bible verse that admonishes you to prioritize your spouse*

   _____

   _____

   _____

   _____

"Experience isn't always the best teacher."

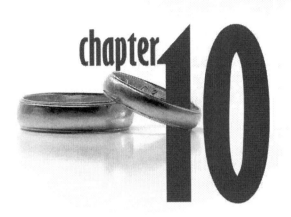

chapter 10

DON'T MAKE OUT, MAKE LOVE

A therapist has a theory that couples who make love once a day are the happiest. So he tests it at a seminar by asking those assembled, "How many people here make love once a day?" Half the people raise their hands, each of them grinning widely. "Once a week?" A third of the audience members raise their hands, their grins a bit less vibrant. "Once a month?" A few hands tepidly go up. Then he asks, "OK, how about once a year?"

One man in the back jumps up and down, jubilantly waving his hands. The therapist is shocked—this disproves his theory. "If you make love only once a year," he asks, "why are you so happy?"

The man yells, "Today's the day!"

I'm not sure whether this expression is still a current expression that people use for sexual activity, but years ago, you heard people say that two young people had "made out" in the back seat of a car somewhere.

God made us and designed sex for procreation. He also made it pleasurable and made it so that the male man and the female will be sexually attracted to each other. However, because God also knew that mankind would sin and pervert their sexuality, He initiated guidelines for the proper practice of the act of sex.

In the book of Leviticus, chapter 18, God delineates the boundaries as it relates to sexual intercourse:

Leviticus 18: 6-26 (TLB)

6 "None of you shall marry a near relative, for I am the Lord. 7 Do not disgrace your father by having intercourse with your mother, 8 nor any other of your father's wives. 9 Do not have intercourse with your sister or half-sister, whether the daughter of your father or your mother, whether brought up in the same household or elsewhere. 10 "You shall not have intercourse with your granddaughter—the daughter of either your son or your daughter—for she is a close relative. 11 You may not have intercourse with a half-sister—your father's wife's daughter; 12 nor your aunt—your father's sister—

because she is so closely related to your father; 13 nor your aunt—your mother's sister—because she is a close relative of your mother; 14 nor your aunt—the wife of your father's brother. 15 "You may not marry your daughter-in-law—your son's wife; 16 nor your brother's wife, for she is your brother's. 17 You may not marry both a woman and her daughter or granddaughter, for they are near relatives, and to do so is horrible wickedness. 18 You shall not marry two sisters, for they will be rivals. However, if your wife dies, then it is all right to marry her sister. 19 "There must be no sexual relationship with a woman who menstruating; 20 nor with anyone else's wife, to defile yourself with her. 21 "You shall not give any of your children to Molech, burning them upon his altar; never profane the name of your God, for I am Jehovah. 22 "Homosexuality is absolutely forbidden, for it is an enormous sin. 23 A man shall have no sexual intercourse with any female animal, thus defiling himself; and a woman must never give herself to a male animal, to mate with it; this is a terrible perversion. 24 "Do not defile yourselves in any of these ways, for these are the things the heathen do; and because they do them, I am going to cast them out from the land into which you are going. 25 That entire country is defiled with this kind of activity; that is why I am punishing the people living there, and will throw them out of the land. 26 You must strictly obey all of my laws and ordinances, and you must not do any of these abominable things; these laws apply both to you who are born in the nation of Israel and to foreigners living among you.

In fact, sex between a couple was legal only within the bounds of matrimony. In the New Testament, **Hebrews 13:4 (NASB) states that marriage is to be held in honor among all, and the marriage bed is to be undefiled; for God, will judge the sexually immoral and adulterers.**

Virginity was expected of both men and women. Today, virginity is looked upon as though it's abnormal, especially if a man is a virgin. We have somehow given our sons the idea that it's okay for men to gain experience before getting married and we turn a blind eye on our young women having pre-marital sex, if they are "wise" enough to avoid becoming pregnant. So, it's a rare thing to find a couple beginning their married lives not having experimented with sex before. Consequently, either the husband or the wife or both come into marriage with a "making out mentality". This "making out" mentality expresses itself in other terms, all of which are based on the selfish gratification of one person at the expense of the other. Sadly, because one or the other spouse believes that he or she is "experienced" because of their premarital affairs, he or she brings the practices, mindsets, and lack of regard for the other that characterized their former experiences.

How can a couple avoid the stress and unhappiness that comes from being unfulfilled in the bedroom? Firstly, you must rethink your perspective of sex. If you came into marriage having had prior harmful experiences such as abuse, rape, and incest, it is imperative that you decide to forgive those who wronged you in that way. If you choose to continue to hate them, you continue to give that person or individual power over you. They continue to keep you captive in your emotions and in your ability to experience the pleasure that God intended you to have in the "holy estate of matrimony". Ask God's forgiveness for all sinful practices of your past and forgive yourself as well.

Wash your mind of unbiblical concepts you picked up from parents, relatives, school friends, adult friends, novels, and the entertainment world so that you will be free for God to make the right impartation to you. If your perspective of sex are still influenced by "blue" movies and other pornographic baggage, your idea as to what is pleasurable will be warped.

Sex should be the most unselfish act between a husband and wife. When both of you come to the "bed" with one goal in mind, that is, to please the other, neither of you will feel cheated at the end. This is God's expectation for married couples. Paul says that both the married man and the married woman's concern is to please the other.

> *1 Corinthians 7:33-34*
>
> *...but the married man is concerned about the affairs of this world, how he can please his wife, and his interests are divided. The unmarried woman or virgin is concerned about the work of the Lord, how she can be holy in both body and spirit. But the married woman is concerned about the affairs of this world, how she can please her husband....*

God is so serious about this covenantal act between husband and wife that He will not allow even prayer and fasting to be used as an excuse to deny each other sexual privileges. This may come as a shock to those of you who believe that you are very "spiritual". God places such priority upon this covenantal act between husband and wife that He commands that married persons must obtain permission from their spouses before embarking upon any prolonged activity of prayer and fasting that will impinge upon their ability to meet the other's sexual needs.

> *1 Corinthians 7:4-5*
>
> *The wife does not have authority over her own body, but the husband. Likewise, the husband does not have authority over his own body, but the wife. <u>Do not deprive one another, except by mutual consent for a limited time, so you may devote yourselves to prayer. Then come together again, so that Satan will not tempt you through your lack of self-control.</u>*

Couples must learn to honestly share their needs with each other.

Become skilled in communicating to your spouse, in a loving way, what is pleasurable to you.

For women who feel that their husband's appetite for frequent love-making is abnormal, allow me to allay your fears. Most men have an insatiable appetite for sex. It's part of their psyche and is inextricably connected to their ego and their drive for success. The best thing a wife can do for her husband when he is dejected because he lost his job or was overlooked for a promotion, is to initiate passionate love-making.

Husbands, on the other hand, must understand that most wives need affection, a sense of security and time if they are to significantly enjoy the act of love-making. Educating yourself on the biology of a woman's body, the psychology of a woman's mind and the versatility of her emotions will go a long way in enabling you to truly be your wife's lover. Experience isn't always the best teacher. I read somewhere that silence does not mean that your sexual performance left her speechless.

There is lot of good, sound, biblical information available today, that can help you avoid the treacherous pitfalls of marital catastrophe. Some of these are listed at the end of this book. You should add them to your library.

REVIEW

1. List some sexual practices that are expressly forbidden by God.

   _____
   _____
   _____

2. What is the best thing a wife can do for her husband if he is despondent?

   _____
   _____

3. Why is a man's sex drive so important?

   _____
   _____

4. What does a husband or wife need to get before embarking on a period of sexual abstinence?

   _____
   _____
   _____

5. What three conditions are important for a woman to fully enjoy love making?

   _____
   _____
   _____

"...what's broken in most relationships is the love verb."

chapter 11

LOVE IS A VERB

Husband: Will you still love me after thirty years when I'm old, fat and balding?

Wife: I do

This book will not be complete if we do not look at a reality that so many couples have experienced......coming to the realization one day that they no longer love each other, or that only one of the two still loves the other.

If they do seek counsel, the common statement is "I just don't love her anymore" or "I just don't feel anything for him anymore". In a nut shell, their love bank is bankrupt. And if you were to take time to look over the chapters of this book, you will discover that neglect, in one or more areas, has brought them to this place.

Usually, if the couple seeks counsel, it is because they still wish to recover what they had before. Whether they admit it or not, they are secretly harboring the hope that whatever is broken in their marriage can still be fixed. But, they are usually operating from the premise that love is a noun. It is something that results from your feelings. If you feel good about the other person, if positive emotions are high… you are in love. But when those emotions are no longer there or at the high you were accustomed to…. you are no longer in love.

Just out of curiosity, I searched to see how many times the word love appeared in the Bible and in my research I found 310 Bible references. What was particularly interesting to me was that out of the first 30 references, only six times was the word "love", used as a noun. Love was a doing word at a ratio of six to one!

This ought to tell us something. It ought to indicate to us that what's broken in most relationships is the love verb. Spouses keep looking for the **result** that comes about from being loved and **neglect to continue doing** the activities that they did in the early stages of their relationship. It was what they did then that made their girlfriend or boyfriend feel loved and caused that person to reciprocate in kind. This is what prompted the question "Will you marry me?" This is what resulted in an enthusiastic, "Yes!" The quickest way therefore, to fall back in love with your spouse is to begin doing and saying the things that you did in the first place.

In the Book of Revelation, Jesus rebuked the church at Ephesus because they had **lost their first love**. He did not suggest that they get a divorce but that they repent and **do** the works that they did at the beginning.

> ***Revelation 2: 4-5***
> *'But I have this against you, that you have left your first love. 'Therefore remember from where you have fallen, and repent and do the deeds you did at first;*

The solution is simple, REMEMBER, REPENT AND REVISIT (do the deeds you did at first). Remember the phone calls, the little gifts, the undivided attention you gave to the conversation, the sacrifice (nothing was too much to do or to ask).

Confess your neglect to your spouse and begin doing again, the things you used to do before. You will start feeling loving towards your spouse once more. If you remain consistent in the activity of loving, you will be blessed with a return.

Our view of love has been seriously influenced by the

entertainment industry. Movies and television shows depict love as transitory and governed by emotions over which we have no control. But there is an element to love that transcends emotions. Love is a choice. We can choose to love, independent of our feelings.

LOVE IS A CHOICE

If love is the servant of our emotions, then God would be unjust to command us to love our enemies. Apparently, God expects us to demonstrate love by our actions independent of our emotions. **Matthew 12:20 "On the contrary, if your enemy is hungry, feed him; if he is thirsty, give him something to drink."** Can you imagine how many marriages would be saved, if spouses chose to treat their spouses in a kind and loving manner despite the contrary emotions that want to rule?

I can almost hear some of you saying that I am too simplistic. What about infidelity you ask? How can I continue to love someone who has been unfaithful to me? Well let me ask you a question, how can God continue to love you when you have been unfaithful to Him?

Please do not judge me as being callous and insensitive to your suffering, to the wounds that you have experienced, and to the nights you have stayed awake questioning yourself; to the revulsion that you feel every time you look at your spouse, and to the humiliation that you relive so many times; to the little deaths you have died daily since you found out.

If I were to counsel you by human logic and reasoning, I would tell you the very thing that you are telling yourself and I would probably vocalize what your family and friends have said. And yes, the Bible does give us a way out with the "adultery" clause. But I will say this. God **permits** you to put away your spouse when adultery or other sexual immorality is involved, but He **does not command** it.

If you can receive it, it is possible for you to forgive a repentant spouse, rebuild the walls of the marriage that have been broken down and to strengthen what remains. It is possible for you have something better than what you started with.

The Bible illustrates this in the story of Hosea and his unfaithful wife. In a culture where a man could put away his wife for any cause, God had Hosea marry a prostitute and take her back repeatedly to demonstrate His love for the nation of Israel. Does He expect any less of those of us who have been brought under the New Testament Covenant?

I've seen couples who chose the way of divorce and I've seen those who chose to forgive and be forgiven, to rebuild trust and to be patient while trust was being rebuilt. I have found that those who chose the latter more difficult path, have often fared better in life than those who did not. This is not to condemn anyone who divorced or was divorced by their spouse. Like Paul, I take the liberty to say that, based on my observation, it is possible to put the pieces together again. Jeremiah 18 gives an account of a potter in whose hand a vessel was marred, but he made another vessel from the marred piece of clay.

A marriage that has stood the test of unfaithfulness, may never be the same again but it is quite possible that it can be better, stronger, and more loving than ever before.

REVIEW

1. What did Jesus tell the church at Ephesus to do when He rebuked them for having lost their first love?

   _____
   _____

2. How can this lesson be applied by couples who feel as though they have fallen out of love?

   _____
   _____
   _____

3. How do we know that we can choose to love even when our feelings are contrary?

   _____
   _____
   _____

4. Is divorce the inevitable outcome of adultery?

   _____
   _____

5. What lesson can we learn from the account of Hosea?

   _____
   _____
   _____

"...no one should enter into this covenant without counsel and carelessly..."

chapter 12
FOR THE BETTER

"What greater thing is there for two human souls, than to feel that they are joined for life–to strengthen each other in all labor, to rest on each other in all sorrow, to minister to each other in silent unspeakable memories at the moment of the last parting?"
– George Eliot

In this chapter you will find an example of the vows that my husband and I designed and use for couples who have decided to be married for the better.

Minister:

Who gives this woman to be married to this man?

Father:

Her mother and I do

Minister:

Ladies and gentlemen, we are gathered here today to be witnesses to the covenanting of (Groom's Name), and (Bride's Name) into the holy state of marriage. The Lord has declared in His Word that this is an honorable estate and He has chosen to elevate it by comparing the relationship between husband and wife to that of His Son, Jesus Christ and His Church. Therefore no one should enter into this covenant without counsel and carelessly for God attaches blessings and curses to the manner in which we treat each other in this covenant. The Word of the Lord in Malachi and in Proverbs charges both the man and the woman not to deal treacherously with the husband and wife of their youth for to do so will invoke the anger of God.

Therefore, I ask you (Groom's Name), and you (Bride's Name) is there any reason, why you should not be joined together today as husband and wife?

I ask those of you, who have come together to witness this ceremony whether you know of any reason, why (Groom's Name), and (Bride's Name) should not be joined together as husband and wife?

Then since there is no objection now, let there be no objection in the future. We shall proceed with the ceremony and as witnesses, you are therefore now responsible to do everything in your power to bless this union, to support this union and to pray for this couple.

Minister:

To Groom:

(Groom's Name), The Scripture declares that it is not good for a man to be alone. And out of all the women you could have chosen, you have chosen (Bride's Name) to be that person with whom you will spend the rest of your life. You have seen something in her that has caused you to choose her above all other women. (Groom's Name), will you always keep that always before you? The Scripture admonishes you to nourish and cherish her, will you fill her life with so much joy, laughter and security that she will never regret the day she married you?

Groom:

I will

Minister:

Women need romance in their relationship. You are her fairy tale come true. Will you continue to provide that romance for her so that she will never have doubt of your love for her?

Groom:

I will

Minister:

Women can be moody at times. Are you man enough not to feel threatened by her moods and not to be irritated by her tears? Can you provide her with loving comfort even when you do not know what she is sad about?

Groom:

I will

Minister:

She needs to know that she can trust you. Are you covenanting with her today to be faithful to her as long as you live? That even though you may feel attracted to other women, you will never allow any other woman to cross that threshold that belongs only to your wife? Will you remain faithful to her as long as you are both alive?

Groom:

I will

Minister:

To Bride:

Something about this young man must have swept you off your feet that you have consented to him to be his wife. Will you promise to always keep that before you?

Bride:

I will

Minister:

The scripture says that he who finds a wife finds something good and that a prudent wife is from the Lord, (Bride's Name) like the prudent woman of Proverbs 31, do you promise to do (Groom's Name), good all the days of his life. Will you admire him, defer to him, honor him and be his biggest fan?

Bride:

I will

Minister:

From today (Groom's Name), becomes your covering, he is your mighty man: do you promise to bring out that might in him,
Will you fill his life with so much love that he will not have any desire to seek for it from any other woman?

Bride:

I will

Minister to Groom:

Please repeat after me

Baby (or whatever term of endearment he customarily calls her) I love you, I really do. As we join hands and gaze into the eyes of each other, I promise before Almighty God and all these witnesses to be the man you dreamt about. I promise to fill your life with so

much love that you will never have reason to seek it anywhere else. I will make your life better. I will be a faithful husband and lover to you. I will be a loving and involved father to the children with whom God will bless us. To the best of my ability, I will provide for you and take care of you. I will be there for you.
This is my promise to you.

Minister to Bride:

Please repeat

Baby, (or whatever term of endearment she customarily calls him) I love you too, and before Almighty God and all these witnesses, I pledge my love to you. I promise to help build you up and not pull you down. I enter into covenant with you to be a faithful wife and a passionate lover. I will help you without nagging you. I will trust your judgment and yield to your headship as you continue to honor the Lord Jesus as your head. I will be a good mother to your children while understanding that they cannot take your place or the attention that belongs to you.

I will give you every reason to realize that you made the best choice in choosing me to be your wife. I promise to fill your life with so much love that you will be too satiated to seek it anywhere else.

Minister to Groom:

(Groom's Name), do you take (Bride's Name) to be your wife from this day forward

Groom:

I do

Minister to Bride:

(Bride's Name) do you accept (Groom's Name), as your husband from this day forward

Bride:

I do

Minister

Ever since people began entering into covenant with each other, there has been an exchange of gifts as a sign of that covenant. What gift have you brought to exchange with each other?

Minister

You have each brought rings. The ring is a wonderful symbol of the nature of the covenant you have entered into. Just as a ring has no ending, even so your love for each other, and your commitment to each other should never come to an end as long as you are both alive.

As you place these rings on each other's finger, please repeat after me.

Groom to Bride:

(Bride's Name), I give you this ring as a symbol of my unending love for you. Wear it proudly as constant reminder that I have entered into covenant with you. With this ring I make you an equal partner of all that I have and will ever possess. What I have now is not all that I will ever have. With you by my side, believing in me, I promise you that you will never lack and in fact you will have more than enough.

Bride to Groom:

(Groom's Name), I give you this ring as a symbol of my unending love for you. Wear it proudly as constant reminder that I have entered into covenant with you. With this ring I make you an equal partner of all that I have and will ever possess. I believe in you that you are going to be a great success and I believe that you will do all within your power to make sure that I will have more than enough.

Pronouncement

Since (Groom's Name), and (Bride's Name) have entered into

covenant with each other and since they have made their vows to each other in the presence of Almighty God and the great cloud of witnesses in Heaven and you, the witnesses here on the earth, and since they have exchanged rings with each other as a token of this covenant, by the authority invested in me by God, I now pronounce that the two shall become one. What therefore God has joined together, we forbid tribulation or distress, things present or things to come, man or women, in-law or outlaw, angel or demon, to separate them from the love of God or from their love for one another.

RECOMMENDED READING:

Covenant Marriage by Gary Chapman

For Men Only by Shaunti and Jeff Feldhahn

For Women Only by Shaunti Feldhahn

His Needs Her Needs by Willard F Harley, Jr

Marriage on the Rock by Jimmy Evans

The Act of Marriage by Tim and Beverly Lahaye

The Five Love Languages by Gary Chapman

The Holy Bible

ABOUT THE AUTHOR

Marcia Judith Estrada was born on the island of Trinidad in the Republic of Trinidad and Tobago. She was born again at the age of eight and has served the Lord faithfully since then.

She and her husband, Apostle Ashley Estrada, have been pastors for over 35 years. They are the founding pastors of Kingdom Life International Christian Center in St. Thomas Virgin Islands and Poinciana, Florida.

Marcia is the mother of five children and four grand-children. She holds a Diploma from the West Indies School of Theology in Trinidad, a Bachelor's Degree in Psychology from the University of the Virgin Islands, St. Thomas and a Masters' Degree in Biblical Counseling from Trinity Seminary. Not only has she authored "The Woman and Her Pastor" book which has helped many churches and individuals but she has ministered in several women's conferences and in leadership conferences and is known for having a powerful anointed word to the Body of Christ in general, and to women in the Body of Christ in particular.

Made in the USA
Columbia, SC
17 January 2018